# Table of Contents

# Women's Voices

A photo of the Walker family taken by Jim Shelton 1918:
*Front row L to R* -John, Margaret, Polly, and Martha,
*Back row L to R*- Nancy, Louisa, Hettie, and Giles Daniel.

C1-0079

C1-0079

Walker Sisters of Little
Greenbrier

# "What more beautiful thing can we see"

A narrow gravel road leads up about a mile from the Little Greenbrier School in the Great Smoky Mountains, past a chortling stream and a forest floor greened with ferns, laurel, and shiny galax. The road swings back into a small clearing where, amid stout boxwoods and filmy apple blossoms, a weathered log cabin remains, as much a part of the landscape as the grand old oak and hickory trees that surround it.

Back in the woods a squirrel chatters busily, a dove croons sweetly, and a woodpecker hammers industriously. But there is another sound, like soft voices in conversation. As you stroll up the path toward the cabin, you might think it's a group of women out on the front porch talking about their day's tasks. Or perhaps they are young girls, teasing each other to be first to the schoolhouse in the morning.

In the small log cabin on this

Edouard E. Exline.

The Walker sisters' home in
Little Greenbrier, circa 1936.

mountain farm, six women lived their entire lives. They were the Walker sisters—Margaret, Polly, Martha, Nancy, Louisa, and Hettie—who spent their childhoods, grew into young women, and lived out their final years here. Six sisters, all born in the nineteenth century, who experienced the joys and comforts and griefs and sorrows that every person eventually knows; who held firmly to their habits and ways even as their century-old family home was surrounded by a new national park; and who through their lives witnessed immense changes in the world beyond.

Today, visitors to Great Smoky Mountains National Park drive into Little Greenbrier, park at the old one-room schoolhouse, and walk up to the Walker place. On a humid day they stir the air with a fan of broad tulip-poplar leaves, recall trips to the cabin when the Walker sisters were still alive, and recollect apple pie warm from the sisters' cookstove, a memory undimmed even after seven decades. They know there's something special about this place, something deeply entwined with the history of these old mountains.

Margaret Jane King and John N. Walker began courting in the 1860s,

*The Walker sisters: L to R* - Martha, Polly, Margaret, Louisa, and Hettie, circa, 1933-35.

*The seven Walker sisters: Front L to R -* Margaret, Louisa, and Polly,
*Back L to R -* Hettie, Martha, Nancy, and Caroline.
This photo, made by Jim Shelton in 1909, is a copy of an earlier photograph.

John Walker with an apple from his orchard sitting in chair that he no doubt made. Taken in 1918 by Jim Shelton.

Pocket knife, side saddle, and powderhorns from the Walker Sisters' Collection, property of the National Park Service. John Walker's powder-horns were made from cows' horns, a material that did not draw in moisture like metal gunpowder holders and repelled rain and snow. The top horn is engraved "1839 J. Walker." Cow's horn was naturally hollow and easily worked, but more importantly, it was spark free.

but their time together was interrupted by the Civil War. John fought for the Union and was held at the Confederacy's notorious Andersonville prison. Upon release, he returned home to the Smoky Mountains, and he and Margaret married in 1866.

They called him "Hairy John" for his snowy chest-length beard, a man who voted Republican and prayed Primitive Baptist. He was known as an excellent carpenter, blacksmith, and orchardist. Margaret possessed her own courage and fortitude, captured in an oft-repeated family story of her response to a commotion out in the henhouse one day. Upon investigation, she found a weasel about to abscond with one of her chickens. She reached down and grabbed the predator, whereupon it latched onto her thumb with full fervor. Margaret proceeded to walk over to the washtub, plunge her hand down in the water, and drown the culprit.

Over the course of twenty-four years, Margaret bore eleven children—seven girls and four boys. The boys married or left home, while one daughter, Sarah Caroline, married. The other girls lived with their father on the farm. John Walker died in 1921, his daughter Nancy ten years later. The remaining five Walker sisters accepted their inheritance and decided to stay on at the old homeplace, partly out of choice and partly out of necessity. These hard-working women put into practice the skills they'd learned from their parents, feeding and clothing themselves, cutting their own wood, raising their own livestock, and maintaining a sustainable farm long after nearly everyone had left the mountains for new homes and jobs in towns.

With five women inside that 20-by 22-foot cabin, things might have felt a bit crowded at times. Though the Walker sisters were most often referred to as a family unit rather than as individuals, each sister assuredly possessed her own personality, talents, and interests, and no doubt a streak of stubbornness and independence at times too.

Margaret Jane, the eldest and her mother's namesake, was born in 1870. Even as a young woman her face was stern in family photographs. The one in charge, Margaret made decisions and the other sisters heeded her word. Stern and practical, she would never engage in frivolous play. Devoutly religious, she led the singing of hymns and often quoted Bible verses. Margaret was reputedly a good marksman and could shear a sheep faster than anyone. While most everyone called her "Miss Margaret," to niece Effie Phipps, Jim and Caroline Shelton's daughter, she was Aunt Margaret. "I loved her, [she was] like a grandma to me," said Effie.

Mary Elizabeth, better known as "Polly," was once engaged but her fiancé died. She was active in the church, and as a younger woman stayed with other people. But she was never able to fully shed her grief. In her later years, she was in ill health, and as Effie Phipps recalled, her Aunt Polly "liked to grieve herself to death."

Third in line was Martha Ann, who also bore the grief of losing her intended. She acted as the family accountant, keeping track of "what they owed and what they paid," said Mrs. Phipps. It was her neat signature, "M.A. Walker," that was penciled on order blanks to Sears, Roebuck, the columns of figures neatly tallied, to be sent parcel post to Route 7, Sevierville, Tenn. At times, she went away for several weeks to work for others. When a writer for the *Saturday Evening Post* came to do a story on the Walker sisters in the 1940s, Martha

Hettie Walker, 1936

Louisa Walker,
photo by Jim Shelton, 1924

Margaret Walker with a rare smile,
circa 1933-35

Martha Walker, 1936

The remaining four Walker sisters (L-R, Louisa, Hettie, Martha, and Margaret) in a ph[...] *Saturday Evening Post* article, 1946.

explained that antique dealers had come knocking, hoping to buy some of their old tools and furniture. But they weren't for sale. In Martha's considered opinion, "What would we do without them? We'd have the money, but what would we work with?"

Nancy was known for her fine hand as a seamstress and needle-

worker, skills that required patience and attention to detail. Paying a supreme compliment, Effie declared that Nancy could make a satin stitch "you couldn't tell which was the wrong side and which was the right side." Plagued by asthma, Nancy stayed inside and did much of the cooking and housework. She was the first Walker sister to pass away, in 1931.

Sister Louisa (pronounced Lou-EYE-za) was "a Jack of all trades and master of none," according to Effie. Poet of the clan, Louisa penned homespun verses extolling her mountain home and was always happy to greet visitors to the Walker home. She was remembered as always smiling and sometimes giggling. But Louisa wasn't just a dreamer—she carried her weight cutting wood and working in the fields. At age eighty herself, Louisa nursed her older sister Margaret in the cabin until she died.

The youngest Walker sister, Hettie, was a cook and a knitter. She knit wool socks for nephews serving in Germany in World War II, and left the homeplace at times to work in a hosiery mill in Knoxville. "She was fun," declared Effie.

Great Smoky Mountains National Park was created in the 1930s, but for thirty more years all five of the Walker sisters, forever in high-necked long dresses and heavy shoes, stayed put and maintained their lives in their beloved mountain home in Little Greenbrier, in what had become known as "Five Sisters Cove."

# My Mountain Home

There's an old weather bettion house
That stands near a wood
With an orchard near by it
For almost one hundred years it has stood

It was my home in infency
It sheltered me in youth
When I tell you I love it
I tell you the truth

For years it has sheltered
By day and night
From the summer's sun heat
And the cold winter blight

But now the park commisioner
Comes all dressed up so gay
Saying this old house of yours
We must now take away

They coax they wheedle
They fret they bark
Saying we have to have this place
For a National Park

For us poor mountain people
They don't have a care
But must a home for
The wolf the lion and the bear

But many of us have a title
That is sure and will hold
To the City of Peace
Where the streets are pure gold

There no lion in its fury
Those pathes ever trod
It is the home of the soul
In the presence of God

When we reach the portles
of glory so fair
The Wolf cannot enter
Neather the lion or bear

And no park Commissioner
Will ever dar
To desturbe or molest
Or take our home from us there.

by Louisa Walker

# The Bear

I have no friendship
With the bear
He will kill your calf
And never a care.

When I am near him
I want him to be asleep
He will sneak to your pasture
And kill your sheep.

Or go to your cornfield
Some early morn
And tear down
A great big field of corn.

Through the thickety hollows
He will crawl
An growl as though
He owns it all.

by Louisa Walker

# A Home and a Farm

*"There is an old weather bettion*

**A**s white settlers poured through the gaps and down the valleys from Virginia into the Smokies in the 1800s, one thing they found in abundance was trees. And the first thing they did was take an ax to those trees and hew them into logs for a cabin.

Among them was John Renfro, who acquired 2,000 acres in Little Greenbrier Cove in Tennessee. He sold 400 of those acres to Brice McFalls in 1838. McFalls cleared a small piece and was likely the first to construct a rough cabin there. In 1853 Wiley King acquired the land and the existing cabin, and began another cabin nearby that his sons completed as a two-room, two-story dwelling.

John N. Walker obtained part of the property and the house when he married Wiley King's daughter, and he acquired more by buying out her brothers and sisters. As John and Margaret's family grew, they were pressed for room. So John took down the old McFalls cabin and put parts of it back together onto the main house to serve as the kitchen. To this "big house" he added a front porch of

14

wide sawn boards, a delightful place to sit on a sultry summer day, shelling peas, paring apples, or spinning yarn.

The hewn logs of the house—some of them seven to eight inches wide—came from massive tulip-poplars. The corners were snugged tightly together with half-dovetail notches, and spaces between the logs were chinked with mud and stones. Wood shake shingles covered the roof, and a wide masonry chimney took up a good portion of the south wall. All rested upon a foundation of sturdy fieldstones.

Every mountain farm included a good share of outbuildings, and the Walkers' 122-acre farm was no different. There was a barn, pig pen, corncrib, smokehouse, apple-house, blacksmith shop, and a small tub mill on Rocky Branch near the cabin. The Walkers never had running water or indoor plumbing (or even an outhouse for that matter). But they were blessed with a clear, flowing spring protected by a springhouse with a stone slab floor. Inside, crocks of milk, butter, and cheese were kept cool and fresh throughout the year.

Hettie in front of the stone fireplace.

A six-foot-wide stone fireplace domi-
nated one wall inside the cabin,
bestowing heat to the living room.
At a second, smaller fireplace in the
kitchen, the sisters did most of the
cooking before they got a wood-
stove. When rain pelted the cabin or
snow flew outside, everyone gathered around the hearth, while a
pone of corn baked and a pot of
beans bubbled with sweet aroma.

The walls were covered with newspapers and magazines; the job of
repapering was an annual chore
that first involved scalding the walls
and applying a flour paste. Frugal
as they were, the sisters hoarded old
catalogs and papers to reuse as wall
covering.

Their father, John N. Walker, was a
skilled craftsmen when it came to
making nearly anything of wood,

*Clockwise from top*: John Walker's .31 caliber percussion rifle with maple stock and Golcher lock. It is likely that John Walker owned more than one rifle. The .31 caliber "squirrel gun" preserved in the park's collection would have been more of a threat than a promise in dealing with bear, but it provided meat for the table and kept many a rabbit out ot the pea patch. Double pocket sewing basket made from white oak splits, cotton gin made by John Walker, split bottom rocker built by John Walker, oak splits basket, commercially made keg.

iron, or leather. He did make most of the furnishings for the house—ladderback chairs, a big kitchen table, fireplace tools, even looms and an innovative small cotton gin. All of these were in the sisters' cabin, along with six feather beds in the downstairs living room and a table, cupboard, flour bin, salt gum, and jelly box in the kitchen. With space at a premium a wide assortment of items hung on the wall or on pegs from the rafters—baskets, hats, lanterns, seed bags, and photographs. Among their most prized possessions was Grandmother King's hope chest and walking stick. "Daddy's" rifle held a place

The ever-thrifty sisters saved just about everything that could be reused. At the time of Louisa's death, th possessions included dozens of seed and other catalogs, including those pictured here. The sisters used newspapers and catalogs to paper the interior walls of their home. This collection shows the sisters kept informed about the latest products of modern agricultural science.

of honor over the door, in case a hungry bear came to root around the hog pen or the corn patch.

The Walker sisters were organic gardeners and guardians of biodiversity long before these ideas became trendy. A gate behind the house opened onto a huge vegetable garden, fenced with hemlock stakes and surrounded by prolific orchards. When the fields needed plowing, the sisters called on a nephew, brother, or brother-in-law who hitched up a pair of oxen or drove "Kit," the creaky Tennessee mule. The soil was good and made better by addition of manure from the stable. But it was rocky ground. Jim Shelton, husband of sister Caroline, recollected "rock piles like hayshocks all over that orchard up there." Old-

Louisa, hoeing the garden. Note seed bag hanging from her waist, 1936.

timers insisted the devil put those rocks there each year to test mortal souls.

Margaret, Martha, and perhaps another sister did the planting and hoeing between hills of corn, cabbage, beans, and potatoes. They saved seeds for the next season, drying and storing them in metal Prince Albert tobacco cans; on dreary winter days they pored over the Burpee and Condon's seed catalogs in anticipation of spring planting time. Reading *Successful Farming* magazine, they gleaned the latest information from agricultural experiment stations. Even with those progressive ideas, they likely paid as much attention to planting in the "signs"—by observing the phases of the moon and the positions of the Zodiac.

The orchards were a sight to behold. John Walker nurtured more than twenty varieties of apples—the ever-popular Red Milams along with what are now considered heirloom types such as Limbertwig, Ben Davis, Red June, Sour John, Abraham, and Buckingham. Peaches, cherries, and plums (wild goose, blue, and Chickasaw varieties), and a grape arbor added to the fruitful abundance. Everyone remembered the Walkers' large chestnut orchard, which produced delectable—and marketable—nuts that could be sold for a handsome four dollars a bushel at Elkmont.

Nearly every mountain farm had a chestnut "orchard," what were really natural stands of trees with the ground kept cleared by grazing cattle. The eastern forest was once full of American chestnut trees— they accounted for more than a third of the woods in the Great Smokies—and all kinds of animals wild and domesticated fattened on the rich nuts each year. But the Walker sisters were among those who witnessed an introduced blight that swept through the forest. It wiped out all the native chestnuts in the Smokies by the late 1930s and spelled the loss of an esteemed wood and a valuable source of income for mountain people.

Honeybees came out of their hollow log hives to buzz about the orchard and among the banquet of blossoms that adorned the Walker place—lilacs, hydrangeas, yuccas (or Adam's needle), pink "grandmother roses," snowball bushes, rose of sharon, and bachelor buttons— more than 100 different kinds of flowers by one person's count. Boxwood shrubs mark the path to the porch, still as firmly rooted in place as the women for whom each

Louisa at the churn and Martha and Hettie behind her on the porch.

one was planted.

Animals were essential on the farm for many reasons. Chickens clucking in the barnyard meant fresh eggs and some meat for the stewpot. From the Holgate Chick Hatchery in Ohio, whose catalog advertised "Baby Chicks—Full of Pep and Bred to Lay," the Walker sisters could have ordered downy hatchlings to replenish their flock. They also had a few ducks and turkeys, along with cows, sheep, and a big old hog or two. The sheep were sheared for wool, cows produced milk and beef, and pigs furnished meat and lard. Livestock mostly had the run of the mountains in summer, but were sheltered in the barn in winter.

Though the Walker sisters' home was relatively small (1,045 square feet), it held an enormous number of possessions. *Clockwise from top right*: Handmade tin corn grater, jug, drinking gourd, homemade keg, commercially-made butter churn, home-made vessel, Dutch oven, iron pot for fireplace cooking, jug.

With the arrival of cold weather, the Walker sisters could rest easy with sides of ham, bacon, and salt pork curing in the smokehouse, and the corncrib packed to the rafters. On any table, pork and corn showed up at nearly every meal. "Everything was flavored with a streak 'o lean," said Robin Goddard, who spent many hours with the sisters when she was growing up. She referred to a piece of lean pork that went into most pots of beans and vegetables. The corn favored by mountain folks was a white variety known as Hickory King—eaten fresh on the cob, ground into meal for cornbread, and fed to animals. When corn got just beyond the roasting ear stage, the Walker cooks also made "gritted" bread—the kernels were shaved from the cob on large homemade metal graters and then baked. To have corn ground into meal, John Walker's tub mill could handle smaller "turns," but for larger quantities they had to go down to John Stinnett's mill. They could get wheat flour there too, for biscuits, dumplings, cakes, and pies. Around the 1940s the sisters had a small hand mill on which they ground corn for their toothless old mule.

From their generous, productive garden, the women enjoyed plenty of fresh food during the growing season. But what couldn't be eaten at harvest had to be preserved for later consumption. In October, said brother-in-law Jim Shelton, "they'd be cuttin' and dryin' fruit, picking up chestnuts in orchards, digging potatoes, pulling fodder, cuttin' tops." Putting food by was no hobby, but an essential task if the women were to eat during the winter. They likely practiced all the techniques known at the time—canning, drying, salting, pickling, and smoking. Sweet potatoes and Irish

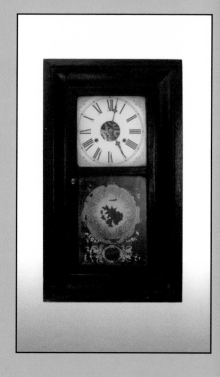

potatoes were kept in floor cellars in front of the fireplaces. "Leather britches" beans were strung and hung to dry, or fresh beans were pickled in barrels of brine. Strips of pumpkin were also dried on poles by the fireplace. Orchard fruits were spread outside on racks or rooftops, and apples were "sulphured" or bleached. Corn, cabbage, peppers, and onions were chopped into tart relish and spicy chowchow, while strawberries, huckleberries, and blackberries were simmered into jewel-toned jams and jellies. When that work was done, the women took their mule into the woods, cut saplings, and sledded them back down to the yard for firewood.

"Our land produces everything we need except sugar, soda, coffee, and salt," the Walker sisters declared. With the modest cash they had on hand, they could purchase

This ornate sewing table (left) is engraved with concentric circles, six-petaled stars, and the words "Clark's Mile-End" (a brand of cotton sewing thread). The drawers have brass knobs and the bottom drawer is divided to hold spools of thread. The clock is a Waterbury mantle clock, circa 1904.

Handmade poplar (tuliptree) corner cupboard. The second and third shelves from the top have plate rails. Whittled pegs are nailed above each set of doors to hold them closed.

Polly, Louisa, and Martha on the front porch of their cabin, 1936

such goods at Jim Metcalf's store down at Metcalf Bottoms on the Little River. During logging days, rolling stores came into the area, and by the 1940s and 1950s the sisters were buying flour, soap, hay, matches, cocoa, and laundry soap from Lawson's Cash Store in Sevierville. Someone may have brought these things to them, or Jim Shelton may have driven the sisters in the car. None of the women ever learned to drive a motor vehicle, but Margaret did take the wagon into Wears Valley.

All the Walker sisters earned reputations as good cooks, especially Margaret and Hettie. Most fondly remembered were their baked cookies, apple pies, and fresh vegetables. At

Fans in the South are most commonly associated with funeral home advertising and were a fixture of country churches. The Walker sisters collection of fans, however, shows a more eclectic taste.

the sound of the dinner horn, everyone gathered for the main midday meal. No one was ever turned away from the Walkers, and if there were too many guests, they would set a second table. For them, food was much more than simply a substance to keep body and soul together—it was a measure of generosity, satisfaction, and kin-ship. Grace was said before every meal, and if Margaret was giving the blessing a person could get hungry before the platters were passed.

During the thin years of the Depression, the Walkers made do like everyone else in the mountains. A cousin living in Missouri wrote in a letter how well he remembered the

"squirl & dumplins" he'd partaken of at their home during that time. At Christmas the delectable aroma of food wafted down the lane from the house, and a person knew he'd be foundering before day was done. The Walker sisters "always had a big Christmas dinner," recalled one. "I haven't tasted a stack cake like theirs in many a year."

The one thing that could detract from the pleasure of a fine meal was the presence of flies. The sisters' resourcefulness glimmered in a clever contraption employed to keep the pesky insects away from the table. As one guest described it, the "fly-brush" was a vertical piece of wood suspended from the ceiling, with a crosspiece extending the width of the table to which strips of newspaper were attached. A diner would pull a string to move the "brush" back and forth across the table, thus warding off flies while they ate.

When the women weren't cooking or farming, a large part of their daily domestic routine involved spinning and weaving. The work of producing yarn and weaving cloth was almost unimaginable, and it took a person of strong character to accomplish it. Said Frances Goodrich, who early recognized the value of this Appalachian craft, "A slack twisted person cannot make a success as a weaver of coverlets. Patience and perseverance are of the first necessity."

Wool began with the sheep. With their father's hand clippers, the

The sisters were prodigious creators of quilts and coverlets. The raw materials for these utilitarian works of art were usually old pieces of clothing, material from cloth bags, and homegrown cotton. The coverlet at lower left is a pinecone bloom pattern signed with Nancy Walker's initials. Because it is two loom-widths wide, it had to be made in two pieces and sewn together. The quilt at lower right is based on a double Irish chain pattern.

Hettie, Martha and Louisa ginning cotton, 1936.

sisters sheared their sheep when temperatures got warm enough in the spring. They would sometimes trim the young lambs, too, for "baby wool." The fleece was washed in lye soap, then combed over and over again with carding tools into soft, silky rolls ready for the spinning wheel. Spinning was a skill gained through much practice, and the Walker sisters kept several wheels spinning for hours on end. Some of the yarn was left in subtle, natural colors, while other skeins were dyed with poke berries or walnut bark. The warp yarn was then threaded onto the big barn loom, so called because it was stored in the barn in winter, that sat out on the front porch in good weather. Shuttles slid

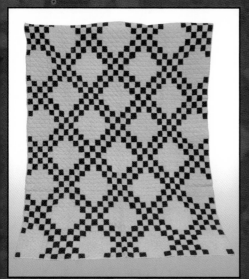

More quilts and coverlets, *clockwise from upper left:* calico quilt with muslin border; muslin-backed patchwork quilt by Margaret J. Walker; small, hand-woven coverlet; double Irish chain patchwork quilt.

The sisters made their own linsey-woolsey cloth from homegrown cotton and wool. Denim and calico could be purchased from mail order catalogs or stores in nearby communities. The brown dress below (*top right*) is made from homespun material, the other two dresses were machine-sewn from store-bought material. The two small bonnets (bottom left and bottom right) are for babies. The light tan bonnet (*center left*) is a child's sunbonnet; the two adult bonnets were designed for wearing while working outside. The burning and aging effects of the sun weren't lost on the Walker sisters. Few mountain women ventured outside uncovered. The bonnet was the best protection whether going to the mill, robbing the hen house, or hoeing corn.

back and forth through these threads, feet worked the treadles, while the weft was tamped down with a steady *thump, thump, thump.* Paper patterns called "drafts" were kept in card boxes, and the Walkers favored traditional Appalachian designs such as Double Knot, Bonaparte's March, and Cat's Tracks and Snail's Trails. The weaver's initials—N M W or M J W—were embroidered modestly in a corner of these fine creations.

The Walker sisters also grew flax and cotton for textiles. To process the cotton, John Walker made a clever small cotton gin of oak with hickory rollers. It took three people to operate—one feeding in the balls of cotton, and one on each side turning the rollers. The fibers of flax were twisted into thread that became the "linsey" of the sturdy homespun cloth called linsey-woolsey.

In later years the women mail-ordered percale and denim for lighter summer clothing. But they stayed loyal to their own linsey-woolsey for winter garments. Dyed in shades of dark blue, brown, and gray, this was the fabric from which they made their skirts, blouses, and aprons, which Martha or Louisa often adorned with a delicate trim of tatted lace. They stitched clothing on a Seamstress treadle sewing machine, one of the first purchased in Sevier County. Using homemade patterns cut from newspaper, with the pieces marked "Dan" or "Jim," they also constructed shirts for their brother Dan Walker and brother-in-law Jim Shelton. Buttonholes were sewn by hand, an art unto itself.

Again, nothing went to waste. Leftover scraps of cloth in brown, red, green, calico, stripes, and plaids furnished the material for pieced crazy quilts and album quilts. Besides providing a creative outlet, quilting was a welcome social affair. Women gathered around the frame at a

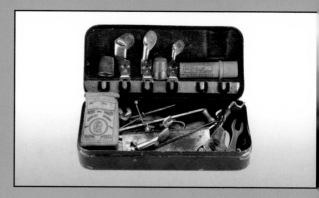

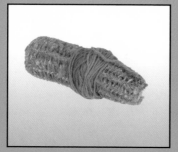

quilting bee and got a chance to catch up on all the local gossip, as they stitched a cherished heirloom.

For their feet, mountain women often found that men's shoes held up much better than women's for working in the fields or tromping to the balds to go berry-picking. The Walker sisters were among those who wore the brown brogans. On their heads, everyday wear called for the classic cotton sunbonnet. But the women did indulge a weakness when it came to hats for dress-up occasions. Among them, they owned quite a collection of fashionable headwear, including cloches in black felt and tulle, bronze velvet, brown straw, even gold lamé, trimmed with flowers, feathers, sequins, and pins. Sears, Roebuck offered such "smart hats at bargain prices," most less than two dollars each.

Sewing was practically a daily task for the Walker sisters. The treadle-powered "Seamstress" sewing machine (*below*) features two drop leaves and wooden casters on legs.

Unbeknownst to most, the Walker Sisters had a passion for modern and stylish hats. Some of their favorites are preserved in the park's artifact collection. Those shown here are made from straw, velvet, and gold lame. They are decorated with grosgrain ribbon, fabric flowers, and glass stone pins.

A surprising array of lotions, potions, and creams were part of the Walker sisters' lives. After the original contents were used up, any vessel was saved for future adaptive use—to store seeds, to mix a favorite remedy in, or

When it came to staying healthy, mountain people turned to herbal medicine and home remedies before they would ever seek out a doctor. Mother Margaret Walker, before she died in 1909, was well known as an herbalist, valuable knowledge that she passed on to her children. In their own herb garden outside the back door, the Walker sisters grew horseradish, boneset, and peppermint for curative teas and poultices. The wild plants of the hills and forest were sought for their healing properties as well—sassafras to build the blood and ragweed to ease the itch of poison ivy. In springtime, they might dig some ramps or down a tonic of sulfur and molasses. Rattlesnakes frequented the grounds, and should a person be so unlucky as to be bitten, the remedy was an application of lamp oil, turpentine, and Roger's liniment. Uncle Charley Walker formulated his own special liniment of Indian turnip and mayapple root; applied externally, a dose was said to cure everything from fainting spells and headaches to stiff muscles and lung problems. Other popular pharmaceuticals included Thedford's Black Draught, a laxative, Wine of Cardui for women's monthly pains, and trusted standbys such as camphor, mentholatum, and milk of magnesia. Still, at times mountain people could do little but watch with sadness as dreaded diseases like flu, croup, whooping cough, and pneumonia took a dear toll on both children and adults.

# Schoolin' and Prayin'

**W**hat book-learning the Walker sisters had in their young lives was gotten mostly in the Little Greenbrier School about a mile from their home. When the teacher rang the bell, they ran down with lunch in a basket (possibly a sweet potato and a leftover biscuit), took their places on the unyielding log benches, faced the blackboard, and read from Webster's Blue Back speller. Their third-grade report cards listed Spelling, Reading, Penmanship, Arithmetic, and Language Exercise as subjects. As for most mountain children, formal schooling occupied only two or three months of the year when farm chores were lighter. And though the Walkers were diligent students, none of the girls went beyond sixth or eighth grade. In those days the value of an education for a young woman was questioned, because people generally assumed she would marry and stay home.

Yet the importance of education was evidenced by the fact that families of the communities joined together to build and support their own schools. John N. Walker and son, James Thomas, were key figures in building the first (and only) schoolhouse at Little Greenbrier. They began work in January 1881, with monstrous tulip-poplar logs hauled by wagon one at a time out of the woods, then split with axes and wedges. Because of his expert construction skills, John Walker was one of four "corner men" who notched and fitted the logs and assured the corners were square.

The first day of school was New

# "To build a house for church and school"

Year's Day 1882, and like every other school day it began with reciting a verse from the Bible and the Lord's Prayer. The Walkers practiced reading verses at home, so they might shine if called upon at school. The distance between school and church was nonexistent back then. Until about 1925, the Little Greenbrier School doubled as a church for local Primitive Baptists, the Walker family among them. When the bell chimed from the belfry, they entered for Sunday school and the main church service, attended camp meetings, or stayed for all-day singing and "dinner on the grounds" where long tables groaned with food. The sisters raised soprano voices in harp-singing, the music read by the shape of the notes in the "Sacred Harp" songbook. Haunting and unadulterated, the old harp songs let the singers express their joy and debt to their Maker. "The Walkers were resilient people," wrote one historian, "who believed that dependence on any strength other than God's or their own was less than wholesome."

Though their upbringing was

41

1909 Little Greenbrier School group, including in the back row, the Walker sisters' brother Giles Daniel and Hettie Walker second from right in the back row.

Little Greenbrier School with Herman G. Matthew and pupils 1936.

strict, the Walker youngsters did enjoy a little playtime. There was a swim in the "frog pond," an event recalled by their Cousin Edith in a 1904 letter she wrote to Nancy from California. Watching beachcombers by the ocean, Edith observed that "it is some larger... than the old frog pond we use [sic] to get licked for playing in... Dear old aunt Margret I wonder if she has forgotten that. I haven't, have you?" The girls did have toys, clever hand-made wooden ones like the gee-haw whimmy diddle, and plain little faceless rag dolls that they loved so much they kept them all their lives.

A hopeful suitor or two did visit the young Walker women, but under the close eye of their father, and then elder sister Margaret, such activity was not encouraged. A corn thrashing or pea shucking was about all the entertainment they had beyond school or church. In later years, they traveled to church conferences around the state.

The Walker sisters undoubtedly were aware of the resorts and hotels in Wears Valley and at Tremont, and of the logging boom that coursed through the Smokies from the early 1900s until the 1930s. The Little River Lumber Company's logging railroad ran from Townsend to Elkmont, and company bigwigs and their guests would ride into the mountains for holidays. The Walkers themselves had a ticket on the train in 1923.

Two years later an earthquake rattled the Little Greenbrier area, and rocks tumbled from the chimney on the Walker cabin. As if a portent of things to come, more earth-shaking changes awaited the sisters, changes greater than they could ever have imagined.

# History of Little Greenbrier School

My father and other men met
In this valley years ago
To build a house for church and school
Where their children could go.

They cut logs in the forest
Though they had no saw mills
The logs were drawn by oxen
Near the foot of the hill

There they were hewn
And notched with care
To build the school house
That now stands there

Yes they all met and
With one accord
To build a house where they
Could meet to worship the Lord.

Though the building of this house
I did not see
Because the schoolhouse
Is older than me.

But I can remember
In my life's early days
How the people would meet
There to sing and to pray

And preachers often spoke
Of a city grand
And a mighty happy meeting
In the promised land.

Most all the builders of
The schoolhouse have gone to God
Let us never forget their labor
Or the path that they trod.

by Louisa Walker

# Little Greenbrier Valley

In the hills of the Smokies
With its towering peaks
With its cool fountains bubbling
And its fast running creeks.

Is a little green valley
With hills on each side
And the beauty of nature
Which no man can hide.

The path through the valley
Goes winding along
Beside the creek
Murmering its song.

With big oak trees
Shading each spot
Where I prayed as a child
Which I've never forgot.

While driving along
this road which I know
You see all kinds of flowers
With their colorful glow.

With the birds in the trees
Singing their sweet song
You see all of these things
Just driving along.

Through the Little Greenbrier
With hills on each side
Is the beauty of Nature
Which no man can hide.

by Louisa Walker

# To Everything a Season

Through the first two decades of the twentieth century, the timber companies had cut wholesale swaths across the virgin forests of the Smokies, removing stately spruce, hemlocks, and hardwoods from thou-

Park superintendent J. Ross Eakin

sands of acres of land. The clank of railroads and the whine of sawmills reverberated through the mountains. Families moved away from their old homeplaces so the men could find jobs in the mobile logging camps, with their company stores, moving pictures, and other new diversions. In addition, the economy was changing from one partly based on barter to one of exchange of cash for goods manufactured far beyond the mountains.

People began to realize the devastation of large-scale logging—not only whole hillsides shorn of trees, but also soil ravaged by erosion and streams choked with sediments. They felt an urgency to save what was left of the green forests and clear mountain streams and to heal the land that had been abused. Men and women met in Tennessee and North Carolina, and in Washington, D.C., to discuss creation of a Great Smoky Mountains National Park and persuade the federal government of the idea's worth. In 1926, with authorization for the park from the U.S. Congress, the two states started raising the money

## "But now the park Commissioner Comes all dressed up so gay"

to acquire close to half a million acres of land, all held in private hands. In the end some 2,000 separate parcels—from small family farms to the extensive holdings of the timber companies—were haggled over and finally purchased. Among them was the 122-acre homestead of the Walker family.

In the early 1930s the Walker sisters began to receive visitors, men in uniform with the new national park, informing them that they, like everyone else, would have to sell their farm and move away. Rooted as they were to their home ground, the five sisters mightily resisted such a thought. A streak of stubbornness or sense of duty may have been involved in their firm stance to stay on at the family home. They might also have

felt fear or insecurity about what the outside world would be like. The prospect of starting over again in a different home and different way of life may have been entirely unappealing, at least to the older sisters. It may also have been a matter of their lack of education, and a sense that as long as they stuck together they would not feel intimidated by outsiders. The sisters had never really wanted or needed much cash money, and they knew well how to take care of themselves. From an immediate standpoint, they may have considered it too disruptive to move their sister Nancy, who at that time was in poor health. Still, all the women may not have been of one mind about the sale of their property

Knoxville Elks Club excursion on a log trestle in the Little River gorge, circa 1911-12. The #9 Shay locomotive would later be destroyed in a 1933 wreck.

A great amount of discussion, argument, and prayer may have taken place in what must have been the most difficult decision of their proud lives.

It has been reported that the Walker sisters initially wanted $15,000 for their property, but the first asking price to appear in correspondence was $7,000. The government got its own appraisals, which varied from $3,500 to more than $5,000. While the dickering continued with the assistance of a lawyer, the sisters took a practical, if not desperate, move to realize some income from their land. They hired someone to cut wood for railroad ties on the farm, and a few years later contracted with a man from Bryson City, North Carolina, to log all the merchantable timber and acid and pulp wood on their land. They were to receive $3 for a thousand board feet of the sawn timber, $1 a cord for the pulp wood, and 75 cents a cord for the acid wood. The logging never took place.

Throughout negotiations with the government, the Walkers wanted a lifetime lease so they could remain in their Little Greenbrier home for the rest of their days. In 1935, park superintendent J. Ross Eakin wrote to the director of the National Park Service that "They are so off the beaten track and it would be considered inhumane here to eject them." That statement was followed, however, with a tougher recommendation: should they reject the government's offer of $3,500, condemnation proceedings should begin.

The sisters held on as long as they could, but in 1940 President Franklin D. Roosevelt stood at Newfound Gap and officially dedicated Great Smoky Mountains National Park. Time had run out. A government memorandum dated

1940, President Franklin D. Roosevelt dedicates Great Smoky Mountains National Park at Newfound Gap.

May 1941 referred to the "acquisition of Tract No. 538 (122.8 acres)... by condemnation proceedings entitled United States v. 122.8 Acres of Land in Sevier County, Tennessee, Margaret Jane Walker, et al." According to the document, the proceedings were conducted and valid title to the tract was vested in the United States of America. In the end the Walker sisters did receive the desired lifetime lease plus $4,750 for their land, approximately $39 an acre. Though the women could stay on for the rest of their lives, park regulations curtailed or ended some of their traditional practices such as hunting and fishing, herb gathering, wood cutting, and livestock grazing.

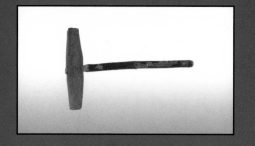

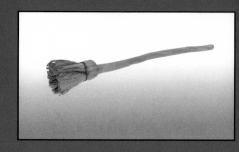

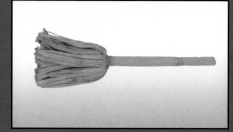

With the national park came more changes that the Walker sisters must have heard of, or possibly even saw, with incredulity. Roads, trails, automobiles, and motorcycles arrived, along with thousands of young men with the Civilian Conservation Corps. With the developments came tens of thousands of hikers, anglers, and sightseers into the mountains. Many of them heard about the curious sisters who lived much as they had in the last century, and some wandered up the old wagon road to the cabin in what became known as Five Sisters Cove. Mostly, the sisters welcomed them, though people remarked that Margaret and Martha could be taciturn and remote. A Knoxville newspaper reported that "visitors found the sisters in the field topping corn, weaving their homespun garments and poke bonnets. But they are not to be disturbed. They are one of the park's greatest assets now."

The newcomers brought with them a source of income that was hard to resist: Louisa sold her illustrated hand-written poems for 25 cents to a dollar, and the other sisters sold miniature toys and brooms, crocheted doilies, and their famed apple stack cakes. Park rangers kept a watchful eye out for them too, lending a hand when they got snowed in. As the land began to reclaim itself, the Walker sisters worried about forest fires and the threat of foxes and hawks marauding among their crops and chickens.

Much notoriety came their way with publication of a lengthy article

*clockwise from top left*: 1). Toy mallet, whittled from poplar (tuliptree) wood and sold to park visitors. 2). One of the tiny replica brooms whittled from hickory by the Walker Sisters and sold to those who visited their cabin. This broom was sold to a visitor for 25¢ in 1955. 3). Replica broom carved from poplar wood. 4). Doll made from cotton scraps, hand-woven cloth, and blue calico. 5). Doll made from scraps of cotton fabric.

in the *Saturday Evening Post* in April 1946, entitled "Time Stood Still in the Smokies." Writer John Maloney observed that "The Walker sisters very definitely are out of this century... as women without menfolk around, they have continued doing things in the ways and with the implements they know best how to use." He went on to describe their solid log home, their dutch-oven cornbread, Martha's apple jelly, "snowy piles" of blankets woven of home-grown wool, their gardens and flowers, the "long-necked" black chickens, and their father's hunting

All four sisters hold a coverlet and pose in front of family pictures hanging on the wall behind them.

Martha, sitting carding wool and Margaret standing at the spinning wheel for the 1946 article "Time Stood Still in the Smokies".

horn, used to signal nearby relatives of any need for assistance.

At the time of the writer's visit, age was beginning to show on the four living Walker sisters: Margaret was seventy-six years old, Martha was sixty-eight, Louisa was sixty-two, and Hettie was fifty-six. Polly had passed away the year before, and Hettie would die a year later. Martha would die in 1951, leaving only Margaret and Louisa to greet people who responded to the "visitors welcome" sign posted near the cabin.

By that time, Smokies visitation was reaching nearly two and a half

Margaret and Louisa in 1962. Margaret was 91 years old and would die eight months later. Louisa was 79.

million people a year. The elderly sisters then wrote to the park superintendent with a request:

*"Will you please have the Sign about the Walker Sisters taken down... the reason I am asking this there is just 2 of the sisters lives at the old House place one is 70 years of age the other is 82... We are not able to do our Work and receive so many visitors... We haven't bin feling very well this winter can't do much at our best... There was 5 of us living here when we began to receive visitors and we enjoyed meeting so many nice people from different places... If we get to feeling better or get till we can receive them again we may want to... but we want to rest a while it is to much work for us now. Come visit us if you have time."*

**Very Respectively**
**The Walker Sisters**
**Margaret and Louisa**

Just before Christmas in 1962, Margaret Walker died at age ninety-two. Louisa stayed on in the house where she was raised, until her death on July 13, 1964. She was eighty-two. Finally, sister Caroline, who had married Jim Shelton, died in 1966. All the Walker sisters are buried in the Mattox Cemetery in Wears Valley, in sight of their beloved Smoky Mountains. Their graves line up atop a grassy hill, carefully tended and adorned with pink plastic flowers. Engraved on each head-stone is the word " S I S T E R."

# Keeping History

Illustration of John N. Walker from one of the best known photos of him.

**F**or another decade the empty Walker cabin and fallow farm began settling into the forest, the trees and vines enfolding it, the years of neglect beginning to show. Effie Phipps, Caroline and

# "When I tell you I love it I tell you the truth"

Jim Shelton's daughter, recalled with fondness her aunts and her grandfather, John N. Walker. Childhood visits to "grandpoppy's" were among the happiest of her life, Effie said. She would sit on his lap while he quoted poetry, always with a moral, often against lying. "He was one of the kindest and one of the best teachers of my life," she said. Of her aunts, the Walker sisters, she professed, "their hearts was pure gold." To the oft-asked question of why they never married, Effie would not venture a guess: "That's a question I can't answer."

From later sojourns to the Walker homestead, Effie was moved to pen a poem that she called "No One to Welcome Me." She wrote of the "visitors welcome" sign replaced with "no trespassing." Absent were friendly hellos or welcoming smiles, no aromas from the kitchen, no bonnets hung on the pegs on the wall. The path was choked with weeds, the garden gate hung on hinges, the corncrib sat vacant. Effie returned to the old cabin as long as she could, reciting her verse from memory to anyone who would listen. She remained one of the firmest voices in favor of preserving the Walker place.

As funds became available, the Park Service began the task of restoration in 1976. With careful documentation by architectural historians, the cabin, springhouse, and corncrib were restored, log by log, with as much of the original materials as possible. In addition, the park has curated some 4,000 possessions of the Walker sisters—including their furniture, spinning wheels, looms, baskets, quilts and coverlets, clothing, papers, and yes, those hats.

The artifacts spark thoughts of what the sisters witnessed during their lives—from horse-and-wagon days, to trains and automobiles, women's suffrage, Prohibition, two world wars, and the coming of the atomic age at Oak Ridge, Tennessee, not so far from their home in Little Greenbrier Cove. The portrayal of them as isolated spinsters frozen in the nineteenth century is too simplistic. Much more than colorful stereotypes, they were human beings with all the complexities that accompany our kind. Certainly the women were aware of what was happening in the wider world and weren't immune to it. They adapted and chose those technological advances that made sense to them—yes to a sewing machine and mail-order catalogs, no to a radio, electricity, and indoor plumbing. They elected to live out of the mainstream of the twentieth century, perhaps because they were content and saw no need to change; perhaps they believed their way was somehow superior to that of a world grown too eager to let go both of material goods and spiritual values; or perhaps the bonds to home and family were just too strong to break.

Finally, it's time to go back up the road to the old homeplace, the lovely, modest log cabin in Little Greenbrier. Walk up to the big front porch, stoop through the low doorways, stand by the big hearth, and imagine how these women, so admirably independent, lived their lives here. And perhaps their voices can still be heard.

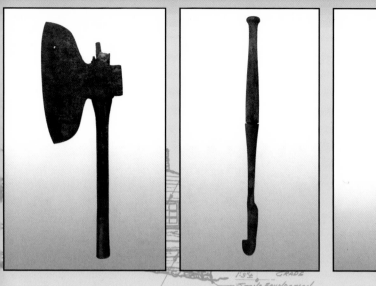

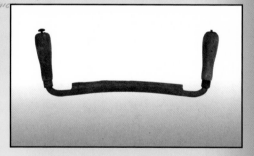

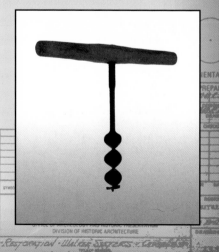

The Walker sisters' collection includes a vast array of tools used for building structures and other woodworking tasks. *From left to right:* 1). Broadax used to hew round logs into square lumber. 2). Barking spud for removing bark from timber. 3). Kraut chopper. 4). Blade for scythe used to cut grass and grains. 5). Drawknife used for shaping wooden objects such as shingles and chair legs. 6). Auger for drilling holes.

## Sources

Brown, Margaret Lynn. *Wild East: A Biography of the Great Smoky Mountains.* University Press of Florida, Gainesville. 2000.
Dykeman, Wilma and Jim Stokely.

"Highland Homeland," in *At Home in the Smokies.* National Park Service Handbook 125. U.S. Department of Interior, Washington, D.C. 1984.

Madden, Robert R. and T. Russell Jones. *Mountain Home: The Walker Family Farmstead.* National Park Service, U.S. Department of Interior, Washington, D.C. 1977.

Maloney, John. "Time Stood Still in the Smokies." *Saturday Evening Post,* April 27, 1946.

Myers, Bonnie Trentham, with Lynda Myers Boyer. *The Walker Sisters: Spirited Women of the Smokies.* Myers & Myers, Maryville, TN. 2004.

Trout, Ed. *Historic Buildings of the Smokies.* Great Smoky Mountains Natural History Association, Gatlinburg, TN. 1995.
Trout, Ed, compiler. Historic Structures Report, Little Greenbrier School. Typescript, Great Smoky Mountains National Park library. No date.

Oral history interviews, Glenn Cardwell with Dan Walker and Jim Shelton; Robert Madden with Jim Shelton. Tape recordings in Great Smoky Mountains National Park library.

Effie Phipps, Landry collection, Video in Great Smoky Mountains National Park library.

## Acknowledgments

Much gratitude goes to Maryann Neubert, Great Smoky Mountains National Park archivist, who took time to go through the large collection of Walker Sisters' artifacts, and to park librarian Annette Hartigan, who made other valuable research materials available. Park historian Kent Cave thoroughly reviewed the manuscript. Steve Kemp at the Great Smoky Mountains Association is the most positive publisher an author could ask for. Many thanks also to Glenn Cardwell, Frances Fox, Bonnie Trentham Myers, Harold Walker, and Kenneth Wise for helpful responses to many questions. Finally great appreciation is extended to Robin Goddard, who graciously and patiently shared her rich memories of the Walker Sisters.

*—RH*

### Walker Sisters Credits

The objects in the Walker Sisters Collection were purchased by Great Smoky Mountains Association (then called Great Smoky Mountains Natural History Association) from the family following the death of Louisa Walker. The Association then donated the collection to the National Park Service. In 2005 the Association funded the photographic documentation of the collection. As part of Great Smoky Mountains National Park's 75th anniversary celebration in 2009, the Association plans to publish a much larger book featuring images of the best of the entire park artifact collection.

Winx CLUB 7

Adventures
Away

# Winx Club
## Volume 7

Winx Club ©2003-2013 Rainbow S.r.l. All Rights Reserved.
Series created by Iginio Straffi www.winxclub.com

Designer • Fawn Lau
Letterer • John Hunt
Editor • Amy Yu

This volume contains material that was originally published in
Italian in Issues 51 and 61 of *Winx Club* magazine.

Printed in China

Published by VIZ Media, LLC
P.O. Box 77010
San Francisco, CA 94107

10 9 8 7 6 5 4 3 2 1
First printing, May 2013

# Winx CLUB

## Table of Contents
### Volume 7

# Meet the Winx Club

Raised on Earth, **BLOOM** had no idea she had magical fairy powers until a chance encounter with Stella. Intelligent and loyal, she is the heart and soul of the Winx Club.

Bloom

Flora

Stella

**FLORA** draws her fairy powers from flowers, plants and nature in general. Sweet and thoughtful, she tends to be the peacemaker in the group.

A princess from Solaria, **STELLA** draws her fairy power from sunlight. Optimistic and carefree, she introduces Bloom to the world of Magix.

Musa

Tecna

Aisha

**MUSA** draws power from the music she plays. She has a natural talent for investigating, and she's got a keen eye for details.

Self-confident and a perfectionist, **TECNA** has a vast knowledge of science, which enables her to create devices that can get her and her friends out of trouble.

Strong and fearless, **AISHA** is able to control the properties of liquids like water. She joined the Winx Club after they saved her from some powerful nightmares.

# Their Friends

Riven

Timmy

Sky

Brandon

## The Specialists

These boys from Red Fountain School are friends with the Winx Club girls and sometimes team up with them to fight trolls and other magical monsters.

# Their Foes

**THE TRIX** are an evil trio of witches from Cloudtower Academy who battle the Winx Club regularly. With leader Icy's freezing powers, Stormy's weather-controlling powers, and Darcy's powers of darkness, these girls love to wreak havoc!

Stormy

Icy

Darcy

# Trouble with Pirates

AT **ALFEA** SCHOOL FOR FAIRIES, THE **WINX CLUB** GET READY FOR A TRIP TO EARTH WITH THE **SPECIALISTS**...

WHOO-HOO! VACATION, HERE WE COME!

BYE-BYE, ALFEA!

I CAN'T WAIT TO HAVE SOME FUN ON EARTH! I'VE HAD ENOUGH OF POTIONS, FAIRY EXERCISES, AND POP QUIZZES!

I CAN'T WAIT TO SEE MY FOLKS! IT'S BEEN AGES!

10

AGHH!!

LOOK OUT!

IS EVERYONE ALL RIGHT?

SHAAA

GASP... I'M FINE...

ME TOO! JUST SOAKING WET... BLECH!

OH, NO! *MUSA!* ARE YOU OKAY?! ANSWER ME!

MUSA'S INJURED! HELP ME LIFT HER, *TIMMY!*

LOOKS LIKE *BRANDON* GOT KNOCKED OUT, TOO!

11

13

HOW ARE MUSA AND BRANDON DOING?

NO VISIBLE INJURIES, BUT SHE'S STILL KNOCKED OUT!

BRANDON'S STILL UNCONSCIOUS TOO...

I WISH WE COULD USE *MAGIC* TO HEAL THEM...

I KNOW, STELLA. I DO, TOO. BUT MAYBE THERE'S SOME MEDICINE THAT WOULD HELP THEM.

TOO BAD WE LEFT ALL OUR SUPPLIES ON THAT AIRCRAFT! WHERE ARE WE, ANYWAY?

THE MIDDLE OF NOWHERE, AS FAR AS I CAN TELL!

LET'S HEAD THAT WAY AND GET BRANDON AND MUSA INTO THE SHADE.

I CAN'T BELIEVE WE'RE SHIPWRECKED!

WHAT ARE WE GOING TO DO ABOUT BRANDON AND MUSA, BLOOM?

YOU KNOW, STELLA, I THINK I MIGHT HAVE AN IDEA.

WINX CLUB, I NEED YOU!

WHAT IS IT, BLOOM?

I KNOW MAGIC CAN'T HEAL THE INJURED, BUT MAYBE IF WE GIVE MUSA AND BRANDON MORE *STRENGTH*, THEY CAN *HEAL* FASTER!

WE'LL TRANSFORM TOGETHER! OKAY, EVERYONE?

WE CAN CERTAINLY TRY IT!

WINX CLUB, TRANSFORM!!

FRIENDSHIP AND LOVE, UNITE AS ONE! LET STRENGTH BE SENT AND HEALING DONE!

NGH... I... I CAN'T KEEP IT UP!

ARE YOU OKAY, STELLA?

I CAN'T SEEM TO CONCENTRATE, EITHER... MY HEAD HURTS!

I CAN'T BELIEVE MY MAGIC'S NOT WORKING!

THIS HAS *NEVER* HAPPENED BEFORE!

IT'S OKAY, STELLA. WE'RE ALL A LITTLE STRESSED OUT. I'M SURE EVERYTHING WILL BE ALL RIGHT.

THANKS, BLOOM...

THE BEST THING WE CAN DO IS TO STAY CALM AND USE OUR HEADS.

RIGHT. WE NEED TO BE STRONG FOR OUR FRIENDS RIGHT NOW.

FIRST THINGS FIRST, GUYS. WE NEED TO DO SOMETHING ABOUT FOOD AND SHELTER.

WE ALSO NEED TO FIGURE OUT WHERE WE ARE EXACTLY...

HOW ABOUT WE SPLIT UP INTO TEAMS?

TIMMY AND TECNA CAN DO SOMETHING ABOUT SHELTER... HELIA AND FLORA CAN TAKE CARE OF FOOD...

RIVEN, CAN YOU COME WITH ME TO SEE IF WE CAN SALVAGE ANYTHING FROM THE AIRCRAFT?

YEAH, BUT...

DON'T WORRY. I'LL TAKE CARE OF MUSA. YOU'LL BE MORE USEFUL HELPING SKY.

OKAY, AISHA.

I'M WITH YOU, SKY!

GOOD!

OKAY, LET'S GO! WE'LL MEET BACK HERE IN TWO HOURS FOR AN UPDATE.

WE NEED TO BUILD SHELTER, BUT IT CAN'T BE TOO FAR FROM THE WATER...

RIGHT. OTHERWISE, WE MIGHT MISS ANY PASSING SHIPS THAT WE CAN SIGNAL FOR HELP!

CAN'T BE TOO CLOSE TO THE WATER EITHER...

THAT'S TRUE. THE WAVES AT HIGH TIDE MIGHT WIPE US OUT!

MAYBE WE SHOULD LOOK FOR HIGHER GROUND...

BRANDON AND MUSA CAN'T BE MOVED TOO FAR, THOUGH. LET'S THINK...

HEY! WE CAN BUILD A HOUSE ON STILTS!

WE CAN USE A GROUP OF PALM TREES THAT ARE CLOSE TOGETHER— SEE?

BUT HOW ARE WE GOING TO BUILD THE HOUSE? WE'LL NEED TOOLS FOR THAT.

YEAH, TRUE. WE HAVE TOOLS IN THE AIRCRAFT... LET'S HOPE SKY AND RIVEN CAN FIND THEM!

20

PHEW! THAT WAS CLOSE!

DID YOU FIND ANYTHING DOWN THERE?

THE EMERGENCY RADIO! IT'S NOT TOO DAMP SINCE IT WAS IN THIS WATERPROOF BAG...

GREAT!

I'M STARTING TO GET HUNGRY... LET'S HOPE HELIA AND FLORA MANAGED TO GET US SOME FOOD!

HELIA, I FOUND SOME COCONUTS!

SHUP

COCONUT MILK IS VERY NUTRITIOUS. IT'LL BE GOOD FOR BRANDON AND MUSA!

NOT ONLY THAT...

...BUT IT'S GOT TO TASTE BETTER THAN *THIS!*

SINCE OUR FAIRY POWERS AREN'T WORKING, WE'LL HAVE TO LIGHT A FIRE THE OLD-FASHIONED WAY...

YEP... BY RUBBING TOGETHER TWO PIECES OF DRY, HARD WOOD!

THERE'S SMOKE COMING OUT!

FUUU

AAAND... WE HAVE FIRE!

YAY! EXCELLENT!!

NOW LET'S GET THIS BONFIRE STARTED!

23

THESE PALM TREE LEAVES ARE GREAT FOR COVER. BRANDON AND MUSA SHOULD BE NICE AND COMFORTABLE NOW...

THIS CRAB IS DELICIOUS!

JUST NEEDED A TOUCH OF SEA SALT! *HA HA...*

THE RADIO SHOULD BE COMPLETELY DRY SOON...

HAVE SOMETHING TO EAT, YOU GUYS. HELIA AND FLORA CAUGHT SOME FISH, TOO!

THANKS, BLOOM.

ARE YOU DOING IT RIGHT?

RIVEN, CALM DOWN. EVERYONE'S STRESSED OUT, BUT IT DOESN'T MEAN WE SHOULD START BLAMING EACH OTHER.

SORRY... I DIDN'T MEAN ANYTHING BY THAT...

MAYBE THE RADIO IS BROKEN.

I ACTUALLY THINK IT'S WORKING FINE! BUT SOMETHING STRANGE IS GOING ON...

I WISH WE COULD FIGURE OUT WHERE WE ARE!

I KNOW... BUT I'M SURE WE'LL GET OUT OF HERE SOON ENOUGH!

IN THE MEANTIME, LET'S TRY AND LOOK AFTER BRANDON AND MUSA AS BEST WE CAN!

SPEAKING OF WHICH, I BETTER GO CHECK ON THEM.

OKAY, I'LL BE RIGHT HERE.

SHFF

RUSTLE

HOW'S MUSA DOING?

SHE WOKE UP A LITTLE WHILE AGO AND EVEN SAID A FEW WORDS. SHE'S RESTING NOW.

THAT'S GREAT NEWS! MAYBE BRANDON WILL GET BETTER SOON TOO!

I HOPE SO!

DID I HEAR YOU SAY MUSA IS BETTER?

YES! BUT SHE'S SLEEPING RIGHT NOW...

I'LL STAY WITH HER. YOU TWO GO GET SOME REST.

THANKS, RIVEN.

GOOD NEWS?

YES! MUSA'S GETTING BETTER! LET'S HOPE BRANDON DOES, TOO!

YOU KNOW, IF I WASN'T SO WORRIED ABOUT THOSE TWO, I'D ACTUALLY THINK GETTING SHIPWRECKED WAS FUN!

SOON, THE WINX CLUB AND THE SPECIALISTS FALL FAST ASLEEP IN THEIR STRANGE SURROUNDINGS...

...UNTIL DAWN BREAKS AND A NEW ADVENTURE BEGINS!

WE'RE GOING TO EXPLORE THE MOUNTAIN AND SEE WHAT WE CAN FIND.

I'LL STAY HERE WITH MUSA AND BRANDON.

WE'RE HOPING TO BRING BACK FOOD, TOO...

FLORA CAN HELP FIND EDIBLE PLANTS. GOOD LUCK!

THE GROUND IS VOLCANIC AROUND HERE!

THAT'S RIGHT! WHICH MEANS...

...THESE ROCKS ARE SUPER STRONG! HERE'S A GOOD PIECE!

LET'S HEAD TO THE TOP TO GET A BETTER IDEA OF WHERE WE ARE.

RIGHT!

WE MIGHT BE ABLE TO SEE SIGNS OF CIVILIZATION... AND GET HELP!

ALMOST THERE...

WATER ALL AROUND... WE'RE DEFINITELY ON AN ISLAND!

AND IT LOOKS LIKE WE'RE ON OUR OWN...

AT LEAST WE HAVE THIS NOW!

TRUE. THAT'LL HELP A LOT. LET'S GET TO WORK!

AND SO, THE WINX CLUB AND THE SPECIALISTS SET TO WORK ON BUILDING TIMMY'S DESIGN...

WHOA... HOLD STILL, HELIA. I ALMOST HAVE THIS LEAF IN PLACE...

OKAY, FLORA.

THIS IS PERFECT! GREAT TEAMWORK, YOU GUYS!

WHAT THE...?!

WHAT IS IT, TIMMY?

A SHIP— A *BIG* SHIP!

THIS IS GREAT NEWS!

QUICK! LET'S TELL THE OTHERS!

SPLASH

WOW! WHAT KIND OF A SHIP IS THAT?

IT LOOKS LIKE AN OLD-FASHIONED SAILING SHIP—A *GALLEON!*

I READ ABOUT THEM IN HISTORY BOOKS! THEY WERE AROUND DURING THE 15TH TO 17TH CENTURY... BUT NOBODY USES THEM NOW...!

SO WHAT DOES THAT MEAN?

HANG ON... IT'S COMING CLOSER...

OH MY GOSH! LOOK AT THEIR FLAG! THEY'RE *PIRATES!*

PIRATES?

THEY LOOT AND STEAL AND CAUSE ALL KINDS OF TROUBLE! BUT LIKE I SAID, THEY SHOULDN'T BE AROUND ANYMORE...NOT ON MODERN-DAY EARTH!

OH, NO! NOW I GET IT!

WHAT DO YOU MEAN, TIMMY?

*THAT'S* WHY WE COULDN'T REACH RED FOUNTAIN EARLIER! WE'VE GONE *BACK IN TIME!*

WHAAAT?!

REMEMBER THAT LIGHTNING THAT HIT US WHEN WE WERE PASSING THROUGH THE DIMENSIONS?

"ITS ENERGY MUST HAVE ALTERED TIME AND SPACE!"

SO AS WE PASSED INTO THE TERRESTRIAL DIMENSION, WE ACTUALLY FELL INTO ANOTHER TIME— IN THE PAST!

WE'LL HAVE TO FIGURE OUT A WAY TO GET BACK TO PRESENT-DAY MAGIX! BUT FOR NOW, WE BETTER HIDE...

"...THE PIRATES ARE LANDING!"

KRSH

UNLOAD ME CARGO, LADS, AND HIDE 'ER IN THE USUAL SPOT!

AYE AYE, CAP'N!

THEY'VE GOT A TREASURE CHEST! THAT MUST BE THEIR HIDING PLACE!

LET'S GO BACK TO OUR CAMP! HURRY!

I HOPE THEY LEAVE US ALONE, BUT WE BETTER BE CAREFUL, JUST IN CASE...

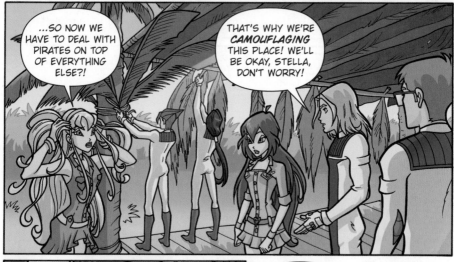

...SO NOW WE HAVE TO DEAL WITH PIRATES ON TOP OF EVERYTHING ELSE?!

THAT'S WHY WE'RE *CAMOUFLAGING* THIS PLACE! WE'LL BE OKAY, STELLA, DON'T WORRY!

UGH! JUST WHEN IS HELP COMING FOR US?

*NO ONE'S* GOING TO COME, STELLA! I TOLD YOU, WE'RE IN THE PAST!

CAN'T YOU SEND SOME SORT OF S.O.S. MESSAGE OUT ANYWAY?

I'D HAVE TO KNOW TODAY'S DATE AND OUR EXACT LOCATION FOR IT TO DO ANY GOOD!

AND OUR RADIO'S BATTERIES ARE SO LOW, WE'D ONLY HAVE ONE SHOT AT IT!

ARGH! THIS IS SO FRUSTRATING!

I'M SORRY, GUYS, BUT I NEED TO GO SOMEWHERE TO CLEAR MY HEAD!

STELLA, WAIT!

SHOULD WE GO AFTER HER?

NAH. LET HER GO BLOW OFF SOME STEAM. IT'LL DO HER GOOD...

LET'S KEEP COVERING UP OUR SHELTER, THEN. IF THE PIRATES SEE IT, WE'LL BE IN BIG TROUBLE!

BUT THE PIRATES HAVE SPOTTED OUR HEROES' FOOTPRINTS IN THE SAND...

CURSES! WE'RE NOT ALONE ON THIS HERE ISLAND!

41

42

43

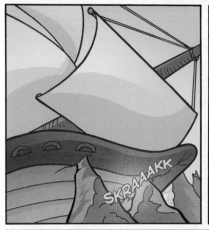

OUR PLAN WORKED, BLOOM!

YES! WINX CLUB—ONE, PIRATES—*ZERO!*

THOSE PIRATES *BETTER* RUN! OR WE'LL GIVE 'EM A DOSE OF MORE *FAIRY MAGIC!*

THAT WAS A GREAT SAVE, YOU GUYS!

I'M SO GLAD EVERYONE'S OKAY, BRANDON!

WELL, THE PIRATES ARE ON LAND, BUT WE'RE STUCK ON THEIR SHIP!

NO WORRIES, SKY. WE'VE GOT PLENTY OF FOOD ON BOARD, AND HELP WILL FINALLY BE ON ITS WAY!

HUH? BUT HOW?

BEFORE LONG...

LOOK! A RED FOUNTAIN AIRCRAFT!

WE'RE OVER HERE!

LET'S GO HOME, GUYS!

STRANGE CREATURE, THAT BE...

MAYHAP ANOTHER MONSTER?

WHOOSH

THOSE PIRATES CAN KEEP THEIR TREASURE— FOREVER!

CAN YOU IMAGINE HAVING ALL THAT MONEY AND NOT A SINGLE MALL TO SPEND IT IN? PURE TORTURE!

HA HA HA!

THE END

# Robot Rebellion

53

54

COMPUTERS DON'T KNOW EVERYTHING— LIKE, HOW GOOD CHOCOLATE TASTES!

HA HA HA! SO TRUE!

I'LL HAVE PIZZA...

OH, MY PHONE... EXCUSE ME!

HELLO?

TECNA, IT'S *IRIS!* I HEARD YOU'RE BACK!

IRIS, HI! IT'S BEEN AGES! WHAT'S UP?

LISTEN, DO YOU THINK WE CAN MEET...*TODAY?* I NEED YOUR ADVICE ON SOMETHING *IMPORTANT...*

SOMETHING *I CAN'T DISCUSS* ON THE PHONE!

55

56

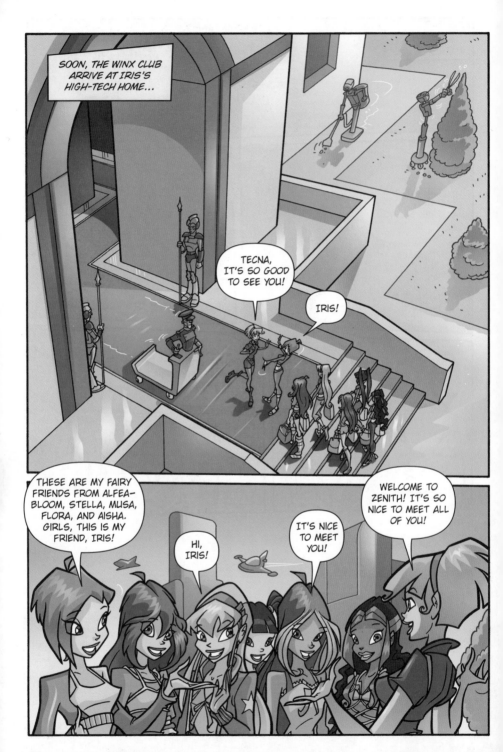

58

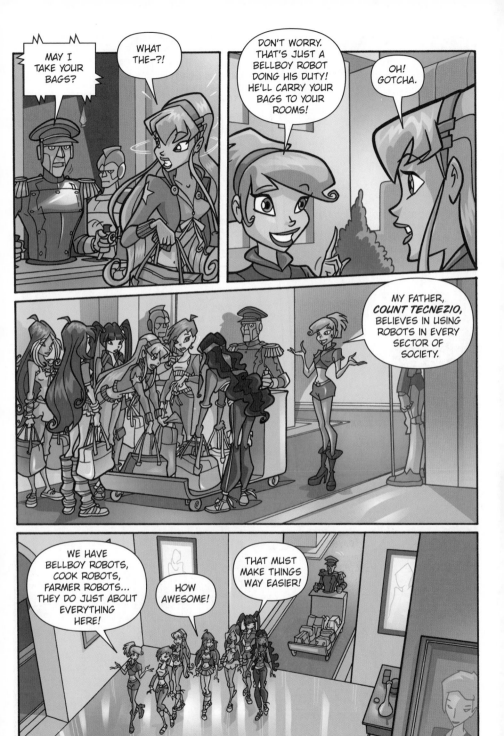

59

ONCE WE'RE UNPACKED, I WANT TO HEAR WHAT'S BEEN BOTHERING YOU.

I'M SO GLAD YOU'RE HERE, TECNA...

I'VE PUT AWAY YOUR CLOTHING IN THE DRAWERS, PROPERLY FOLDED.

WHAT?! REALLY?!

I'VE ALSO ADJUSTED THE SHOWER TO 10 DEGREES ABOVE YOUR BODY TEMPERATURE, AND YOUR FAVORITE SHAMPOOS ARE READY FOR USE.

THAT'S TOTALLY AWESOME!!

WAIT... HOW DID HE KNOW MY FAVORITE SHAMPOO?

HE HAS A BUILT-IN SCANNER THAT IDENTIFIED THE SHAMPOO YOU USE IN YOUR HAIR!

WHOA! THIS IS SERIOUS TECHNOLOGY!

YOU CAN SEE WHY WE CAN'T LIVE WITHOUT OUR ROBOTS.

THEY HELP THE ELDERLY, TAKE CARE OF THE SICK, CULTIVATE THE LAND...

IT'S A PLEASURE TO MEET YOU, PRINCESS STELLA OF SOLARIA!

BUT... HOW DO YOU KNOW WHO I AM?

THE AIRPORT TRANSMITTED YOUR DATA. I MEMORIZED IT, WITH RESPECT FOR YOUR PRIVACY, OF COURSE...

YOU CAN ERASE YOUR DATA FROM MY MEMORY AT ANY TIME, IF YOU LIKE.

WELL... WHAT ELSE DO YOU KNOW ABOUT ME?

YOU GO TO SCHOOL AT ALFEA, WHERE YOU DO WELL AND ARE A MEMBER OF THE WINX CLUB. YOU ALSO LOVE SILK TOPS BY FRISKAR.

WOW... THAT'S TOTALLY TRUE!

THIS YEAR'S COLLECTION IS MAGNIFICENT. THE SUN-YELLOW BEADED TOP IN PARTICULAR IS REMARKABLE.

OH, YES! I'VE SEEN IT! IT'S MY FAVORITE!

DID YOU GUYS HEAR THAT? HE'S INCREDIBLE!

ROBOTS LIKE MEMOX HAVE AMAZING ABILITIES— AND HE'S TOP OF THE LINE!

64

I SENSE THAT YOU STILL HAVE A SLIGHT FEVER, MY LADY. YOU MUST TAKE CARE OF YOURSELF AND NOT WORRY SO MUCH.

I'LL BE FINE, BUT I APPRECIATE YOUR CONCERN.

I HAVE TO FINISH SOME ACCOUNTING, SO DO EXCUSE ME. IF YOU NEED ANYTHING, PLEASE CALL.

IT WAS NICE TO MEET YOU, MEMOX!

WILL DO.

I'D *LOVE* TO HAVE A ROBOT LIKE HIM!

SHHHH!

SO YOU'VE BEEN SICK, IRIS? WHAT'S BEEN WORRYING YOU?

I FEEL LIKE I CAN TRUST THE WINX CLUB WITH THIS AS WELL, SO I'LL TELL YOU...

67

IT'S A BOOK OF POEMS MEMOX WROTE FOR ME! THEY'RE BEAUTIFUL!

A ROBOT CAN WRITE POEMS?

YES! MEMOX IS KINDER, AND MORE INTELLIGENT THAN MANY PEOPLE I KNOW... HE'S ALMOST HUMAN!

BUT IF THIS ROBOT REBELLION HAPPENS...ALL HUMANS COULD BE IN BIG TROUBLE!

WHAT DOES YOUR FATHER SAY?

ON THE ONE HAND, HE'S FASCINATED BY THE ROBOTS' ABILITY TO DEVELOP THEIR OWN PERSONALITIES...

...BUT ON THE OTHER HAND, HE'S VERY CONCERNED ABOUT THE SAFETY OF HIS REALM. HE'S PUT THE ARMY ON FULL ALERT!

I SEE...

I JUST REALLY NEEDED TO CONFIDE IN SOMEONE...

OF COURSE, IRIS. WE'RE *ALL* HAPPY TO HELP!

WE'LL SEE IF WE CAN THINK OF A WAY TO HELP CALM THINGS DOWN!

THANKS SO MUCH, TECNA...

I'LL LET YOU GUYS RELAX NOW. SEE YOU AT DINNER!

SOUNDS GOOD!

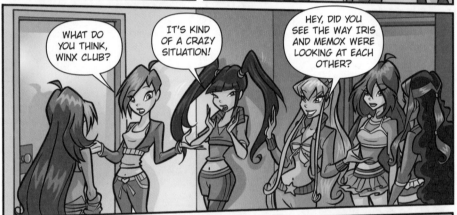

WHAT DO YOU THINK, WINX CLUB?

IT'S KIND OF A CRAZY SITUATION!

HEY, DID YOU SEE THE WAY IRIS AND MEMOX WERE LOOKING AT EACH OTHER?

I THINK SHE'S GOT IT BAD! HE EVEN WRITES POEMS TO HER! CAN YOU BELIEVE IT?

COME ON, STELLA... DON'T START!

WELL, I CAN SEE STELLA'S POINT... IT'S EASY TO FALL FOR SOMEONE WHO REALLY UNDERSTANDS YOU... THAT'S WHAT HE DOES FOR HER, RIGHT?

BUT, FLORA... HE'S A *ROBOT!*

71

HEY! THE LIGHTS WENT OUT!

AND THE SHOWER STOPPED WORKING! MY HAIR'S STILL FULL OF SHAMPOO!

SO MUCH FOR THE WONDERS OF TECHNOLOGY... BLECH!

GIRLS, OPEN UP! IT'S IRIS!

NOK NOK NOK

IRIS, WHAT'S GOING ON?

THE REBELLION JUST BROKE OUT! THE ROBOTS ARE *GONE!*

WHAT?

THEY'VE ALL LEFT THE MANSION, EVEN MEMOX! AND THEY CUT THE ELECTRICITY WHEN THEY LEFT!

MEMOX TOO? SO HE'S A PART OF THE REBELLION...?

UGH... WHAT AM I GOING TO DO ABOUT MY HAIR?

I'M NOT SURE IF MEMOX WENT WITH THEM WILLINGLY OR IF HE WAS FORCED TO GO... I DON'T KNOW WHAT TO THINK!

SO I'M GOING TO HAVE BAD HAIR DAYS UNTIL THIS REBELLION IS OVER?!

WELL, THE EMERGENCY GENERATORS SHOULD BE UP AND RUNNING SOON...THERE WE GO!

WHRRRRUMM

PHEW! THE ELECTRICITY'S BACK!

THANK GOODNESS!

WITHOUT ROBOTS, IT'S GOING TO BE A LONG DAY! WE'LL HAVE TO DO THEIR CHORES...

WHAT KIND OF CHORES?

WELL, WE HAVE TO COOK, WASH, CLEAN... THE ROBOTS USED TO DO ALL THAT!

WE'LL ALL DO OUR PART, IRIS! YOU CAN COUNT ON US!

73

74

HMM... WELL, MAYBE THAT'S WHAT I'LL USE!

YOU KNOW THAT I WANTED A BEAUTIFUL BIRD... SO JUST GET GOING, YOU KNOW WHAT YOU HEARD!

VOILÀ! TRY IT!

UH... NO, THANKS.

GIVE IT A TASTE YOURSELF, STELLA.

PUH! IT TASTES GROSS!

I GUESS IF YOU DON'T KNOW HOW TO COOK, NOT EVEN MAGIC WILL FIX FLAVORS!

WELL, I'M *NOT* A COOK! AND I DON'T EVEN WANT TO *THINK* ABOUT WASHING DISHES...

HOW ABOUT I PUT ALL THE POTS AND PANS IN ORDER? THAT'S HELPFUL, RIGHT?

TOTALLY...AS LONG AS YOU DON'T COOK ANYTHING ELSE IN THEM!

77

MEMOX CAME HERE TO WARN ME...BUT TWO REBEL ROBOTS JUST CAPTURED HIM AND TOOK OFF!

WHAT?!

WHY DON'T WE GET THE ARMY TO RESCUE HIM?

THEY'VE GOT TO GUARD THE CITY, STELLA...

THE WINX CLUB WILL HELP OUT WITH THIS, IRIS, DON'T WORRY!

I BET *WE* COULD RESCUE MEMOX...

IRIS, DO YOU KNOW WHERE THEY WERE TAKING HIM?

WELL, MEMOX SAID THE ROBOT REBELS ARE HIDING IN THE MOUNTAINS...

GOOD! THEN WE'LL HEAD THERE AND TRY TO SET HIM FREE!

BUT HOW ARE YOU GOING TO GET THERE? OUR AIRCRAFT ARE ALL GROUNDED WITHOUT ROBOTS TO FLY THEM!

WE'RE *FAIRIES*, IRIS! *FLYING* THERE IS GOING TO BE A SNAP!

I'LL POSE AS A ROBOT BRINGING A CAPTURED HUMAN TO THE PRISON, GET IT?

I'LL BE THE PRISONER!

ARE YOU SURE, IRIS? IT MIGHT BE BETTER FOR ANOTHER WINX CLUB GIRL TO GO WITH TECNA...

NO, I'LL DO IT!

I'LL TIE YOU UP WITH THESE WEAK VINES THEN. YOU'LL BE ABLE TO GET OUT OF THEM EASILY!

STAND BY IN CASE WE NEED YOU!

WILL DO! GOOD LUCK!

HALT! WHO GOES THERE?

I CAPTURED A HUMAN SPY! I'M TAKING HER TO THE PRISON!

MULTIMAX WILL WANT TO QUESTION HER, BUT SHE MUST BE DETAINED IN THE MEANTIME.

GOOD! THIS IS THE RIGHT PLACE!

PUT HER IN THE FIRST FREE CELL AT THE BACK OF THE CAVE.

GOT IT!

WE DID IT, TECNA! WE'RE IN!

GETTING *OUT* WILL BE THE HARD PART... LET'S HURRY UP AND FIND MEMOX!

...IT WAS A *SERIOUS MISTAKE*, BUT THERE'S STILL A WAY TO FIX THINGS.

THAT'S MEMOX'S VOICE!

SO IF YOU'LL SUPPORT ME WHEN I TALK TO MULTIMAX...

DEFINITELY!

COUNT ME IN, TOO!

86

87

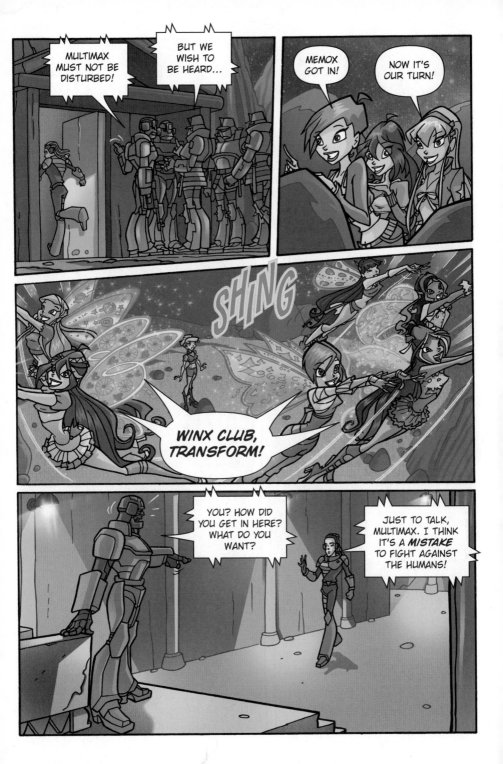

90

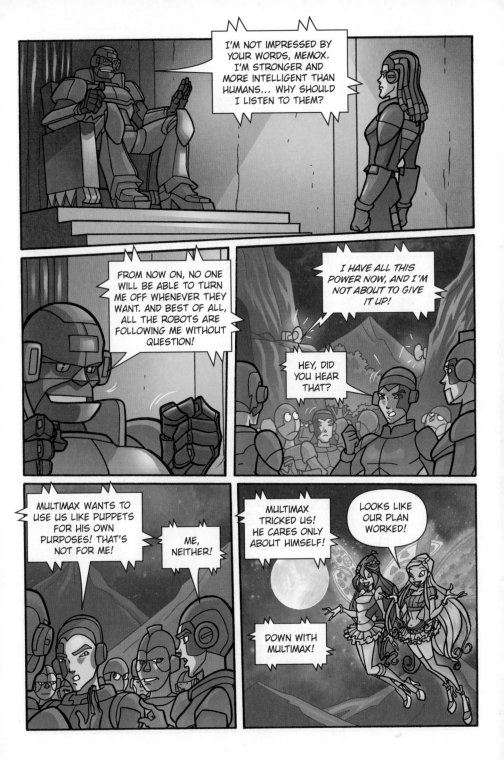

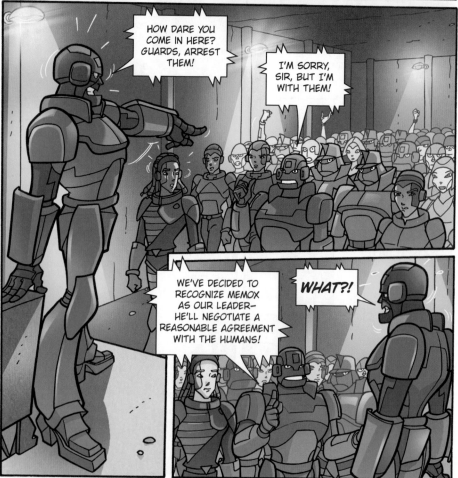

...AND THE WINX CLUB HAD A FRONT-ROW SEAT!

YAAAAY!!

ROBOTS WHO WISHED TO LIVE ON THEIR OWN COULD NOW DO SO...

...WHILE OTHERS LOOKED FORWARD TO RETURNING TO THEIR HOMES WITH HUMANS...

95